TREASURE HUNTERS

PIRATE TREASURE

NICK HUNTER

Chicago, Illinois

Edited by Laura Knowles, Adam Miller, Harriet Milles, and Helen Cox Cannons
Designed by Victoria Allen
Original illustrations © Capstone Global Library Ltd 2013
Illustrated by Martin Bustamante
Picture research by Tracy Cummins

Originated by Capstone Global Library Ltd.
Production by Alison Parsons
Printed and bound in China by Leo Paper Products Ltd

16 15 14 13 12
10 9 8 7 6 5 4 3 2 1

Library of Congress Cataloging-in-Publication Data
Hunter, Nick.
    Pirate treasure / Nick Hunter.
        p. cm.—(Treasure hunters)
    Includes bibliographical references and index.
    ISBN 978-1-4109-4953-0 (hb)—ISBN 978-1-4109-4960-8 (pb) 1. Treasure troves—Juvenile literature. 2. Pirates—Juvenile literature. I. Title.
    G525.H8975 2013
    910.4'5—dc23   2012012890

Acknowledgments
We would like to thank the following for permission to reproduce photographs: Alamy pp.11 (©Mary Evans Picture Library), 13, 14, 39 (©North Wind Picture Archives); AP Photo pp.24 (The News & Observer, Robert Willett), 25 (The Jacksonville Daily News, Chuck Beckley); Art Resources p.23 (The Art Archive /Anthony Hilder); Corbis pp.5 (©Lebrecht Music & Arts), 15 (©Bettmann), 27 bot (©Rick Friedman), 33 bot (©Richard T. Nowitz), 41 (©Stefano Bianchetti), 43 (©Ocean); Getty Images pp.6 top (Paul Popper/Popperfoto), 9 bot (Mansell/Time & Life Pictures), 12 mid (Fotosearch), 19 (Hulton Archive), 21 (The Bridgeman Art Library), 40 top (Don Farrall); Library of Congress Prints and Photographs Division p.30; NASA p.20; National Geographic Stock p.17 (©NickCaloyianis/inspection by Chris Macort); oakislandtreasure.co.uk pp.34 (Jo Atherton), 36, 37 (D'Arcy O'Connor); Shutterstock pp.1 bot (Linda Bucklin), 1 top (Albert Campbell), 4 bot (Fer Gregory), 4 top (il67), 6 bot (AVprophoto), 6 bot (Amitofo), 7 bot (ChromaCo), 8 bot (ULKASTUDIO), 8 top (KTS7077), 10 (africa924), 12 bot (prochasson Frederic), 12 top (Molodec), 16 (Zavodskov Anatoliy Nikolaevich), 18 (PLRANG), 22 (koya979), 26 (Marcus Efler), 27 top (Triff), 31 bot (kokitom), 31 top (ChromaCo), 32 bot (DEKANARYAS), 32 mid (LoopAll), 32 top (Christopher Brewer), 33 top (James Steidl), 35 (ronstik), 38 left (Igrik), 38 right (shutswis), 40 bot (Iakov Filimonov), 42 (Maugli); Superstock pp.7 top (©SuperStock), 9 top (©Loop Images). Design features: ©Shutterstock.

Cover photographs reproduced with permission of Getty Images (©Dariush M.), Getty Images (©Colin Anderson), and Shutterstock (©Massimo Saivezzo).

Every effort has been made to contact copyright holders of material reproduced in this book. Any omissions will be rectified in subsequent printings if notice is given to the publisher.

Expert consultant
We would like to thank Dr. David J. Starkey for his invaluable help in the preparation of this book. Dr. Starkey is director of the Maritime Historical Studies Center, head of the Department of History at the University of Hull, England, and editor of the *International Journal of Maritime History*.

Guided Reading Level: V

CONTENTS

OCEAN RAIDERS

Imagine you are sailing on the open sea, far from land, when all of a sudden a chill runs down your spine: the ship coming toward you has just raised a skull and crossbones flag!

This was once a real possibility for sailors crossing the world's oceans on ships carrying goods for trade, passengers, and treasure. Sailors lived in fear of pirates. A ship might appear on the horizon that looked friendly. As it got closer, the crew of the merchant ship would be terrified to see a black pirate flag raised to the top of the mast and armed men crowding the rail of the pirate ship, ready to take their treasure and kill anyone who resisted!

Pirates have been around since people first sailed the seas. They often have a glamorous reputation, but in most cases they were gangs of robbers who attacked any ship that came their way, caring little about whom they had to murder to get their hands on the loot.

TALES OF TREASURE

Over the centuries, legends have grown about the fabulous treasures of pirates such as Blackbeard and Captain Kidd. Most of these treasures have never been found. They could still be out there somewhere, beneath the sea or buried on desert islands—waiting to be discovered by modern treasure hunters.

Most pirates were men, but there were some famous women pirates. Anne Bonny and Mary Read dressed as men to terrorize ships in the Caribbean.

CORSAIRS AND PRIVATEERS

The earliest known pirates terrorized the trading routes of the Mediterranean Sea more than 2,000 years ago. From ancient Greek raiders to the corsairs of North Africa, who ruled the seas after 1000 CE, these pirates were mainly interested in a particular kind of treasure—people. They could make money by capturing sailors and other travelers and selling them as slaves, or by releasing them in return for a ransom.

The Barbarossa brothers raided ships along the coast of North Africa in the 1500s.

HORUSCE und HAREADEN BARBAROSSA
Könige von Tunis und Algiers, und ober See Admiralen.

Wealthy victims of the North African corsairs would swallow their jewelry to avoid handing it over. The crafty pirates fed them a mixture that made them need to go to the bathroom-- and reveal the treasure!

OFFICIAL PIRATES

During the 1500s, great riches started to come to Europe from Central and South America. The golden treasures of the Inca civilization were melted down by Spanish invaders and transported back across the Atlantic Ocean. They were sometimes attacked by privately owned ships licensed by governments to capture enemy ships and their cargoes. These licensed ships were known as privateers. The most famous English privateer captain was Francis Drake, who gave part of his treasure to Queen Elizabeth I of England.

Barbary corsairs and privateers did not bury their treasure. Instead, they used it to make themselves wealthy and respected citizens. However, later pirates lived outside the law and would attack ships of every nation.

FRANCIS DRAKE

Born: c. 1543, Died: 1596

Nationality: English

In addition to raiding Spanish ships and stealing their treasure, Drake was also the first Englishman to sail around the world. He was knighted by Queen Elizabeth I, who called him her "pirate."

FACT VERSUS FICTION

The traditional image of the pirate mostly comes from the Golden Age of Piracy. During the late 1600s and early 1700s, pirate ships roamed the coasts and islands from the Caribbean to the Indian Ocean. These pirates came from many European nations, in addition to outlaws and runaway slaves from the coastal colonies of North America.

Stories of pirates and their treasure have been told for almost as long as there have been pirates. Some famous examples are Robert Louis Stevenson's book *Treasure Island* and J. M. Barrie's *Peter Pan*. These stories have led to many of the myths about pirates.

Test your swashbuckling knowledge!

Do you know the difference between pirate fact and fiction? Which of these statements do you think are true?

1. Pirates made people walk the plank as a punishment.

2. Pirates kept parrots as pets.

3. There was only one Jolly Roger pirate flag.

4. Pirates really buried their treasure.

Answers: (1) False—this is a myth! (2) True—parrots were exotic birds that were unknown in Europe at the time. (3) False—there were many different Jolly Roger designs. Today, the skull and crossbones is the most famous. (4) Maybe—experts disagree!

The Jolly Roger represented death and struck fear into the pirates' victims.

Pirate technology

Having the right technology meant that pirates could catch their targets while also avoiding the ships that tried to catch them. Ships like Captain Kidd's *Adventure Galley* had to be as fast as the latest warships. Pirates used local knowledge to know where to lie in wait for treasure ships. If they could steal a chart, or map, of the coast from a Spanish galleon, that was as valuable as any treasure.

Spanish fleets had to be on the lookout for attacks from pirates.

CAPTAIN KIDD'S TREASURE

By the late 1600s, there was less treasure for pirates to seize in the Caribbean. They looked elsewhere for riches. The Indian Ocean was home to the treasure ships of Arab and Indian rulers, as well as European trading ships carrying valuable goods from the East.

Pirates such as Henry Avery and Thomas Tew terrorized ships in the Indian Ocean, returning to their bases in North America with rich treasures. Powerful merchants wanted these pirates stopped and so, in 1695, a group of English backers provided money for a new ship to capture the pirates. The leader of this mission was Captain William Kidd.

Madagascar, an island off the coast of Africa, was a perfect base for the pirates who roamed the Indian Ocean.

THREAT OF MUTINY

Kidd's ship *Adventure Galley* searched the Indian Ocean for pirates and their treasure but, when they failed to find them, the crew grew tired of eating rotten food and drinking foul water. They had signed on with the promise of treasure. The crew members threatened mutiny as Kidd refused to attack an English merchant ship.

CAPTAIN WILLIAM KIDD

Born: c. 1645

Died: 1701

Nationality: Scottish

Captain Kidd could have lived a comfortable life as a wealthy New York merchant, but his love of the sea led him to become a pirate captain.

One of the pirates Kidd followed to the Indian Ocean was Henry Avery. Avery's capture of a Mughal treasure ship was possibly the richest pirate raid in history. Despite his success, Avery died in poverty.

THE QUEDAGH MERCHANT

Finally, Kidd and his crew found the prize they were looking for. The *Quedagh Merchant* was an Armenian trading ship piled high with treasure. Kidd turned from pirate hunter to pirate. His men boarded the ship and seized its cargo of gold, silk, and spices worth over $11 million in today's money.

THE UNLUCKY PIRATE

Kidd had made his fortune, but now his luck started to run out. He took his prize to Madagascar, where many of his crew joined a rival pirate. Kidd was a wanted man by the time he returned to the Caribbean in the *Quedagh Merchant*. He abandoned the ship and fled to Long Island in New York, hoping that the political backers who had funded his mission would protect him—but he was caught, tried, and hanged.

THE
Arraignment, Tryal, and Condemnation
OF
Captain William Kidd,
FOR
MURTHER
AND
PIRACY,
Upon Six feveral Indictments,

At the Admiralty-Seffions, held by His Majefty's Commiffion at the *Old-Baily*, on *Thurfday* the 8th. and *Friday* the 9th. of *May*, 1701. who, upon full Evidence, was found Guilty, receiv'd Sentence, and was accordingly Executed at *Execution-Dock*, *May* the 23d.

AS ALSO,
The TRYALS of *Nicholas Churchill*, *James Howe*, *Robert* ... *William Jenkins*, *Gabriel Loff*, *Hugh Parrot*, *Richard Barlicorn*, ... *Mullins*, at the fame Time and Place

Kidd left the *Quedagh Merchant* in Hispaniola, an island that was home to many of the most feared pirates.

Even Captain Kidd's execution did not go smoothly. The first rope used to hang him snapped and he had to be hanged again.

After being hanged in front of a big crowd, Kidd's body was hung from a gibbet beside England's Thames River for two years, as a warning to others.

HUNT

There are many stories about Captain Kidd's mission to the Indian Ocean and those who funded it. The biggest legend of all was about Kidd's treasure. We know that Kidd buried boxes of gold and other treasure on Gardiner's Island, near New York City. This treasure was found soon after Kidd's capture, but did Kidd bury treasure anywhere else?

MAP MYSTERY?

In 1929, Hubert Palmer bought a desk that was said to belong to Captain Kidd. In it, he found a map bearing Kidd's initials and showing an island in the China Sea. In the years that followed, Palmer discovered other maps hidden in furniture belonging to Kidd. These maps seemed to date from the right time, but there were errors in dates and other details that led many to question whether they were genuine. If the maps are real, where is the island they refer to?

The search for Kidd's treasure continues. Islands in the South China Sea and Oak Island, in Nova Scotia, Canada, have been claimed as the home of his treasure.

Captain Kidd burying his treasure on Gardiner's Island.

Captain Kidd's treasure maps

Just because a document says that it belonged to Captain Kidd does not make it genuine. Researchers can analyze paper, ink, and even the spelling used to decide if a document was made at the right time. Even if the treasure maps date from the right time, it is very difficult to prove they belonged to Captain Kidd.

This note from Captain Kidd was signed just before his death in 1701. Could Kidd's treasure map really have remained hidden for so long?

IN SEARCH OF CAPTAIN KIDD

The trail of Captain Kidd's treasure seemed to have gone cold until 2007. Then, researchers from Indiana University found a ship in shallow water in the Dominican Republic, which now covers part of the island of Hispaniola. After studying the remains of the ship and comparing them to documents from the time, they believed that they had found the remains of Captain Kidd's *Quedagh Merchant*.

The *Quedagh Merchant* remained undiscovered for more than 300 years in just 10 feet (3 meters) of water.

Kidd had abandoned the ship when he fled to New York. Researchers believe that his crew looted the ship, started a fire, and set the boat adrift. The remains that have been found include several cannons and anchors. However, Kidd and the crew almost certainly took any treasure with them.

Charles Beeker led the team that found the remains of the *Quedagh Merchant*. He said that when he first saw the shipwreck, he could not believe that everybody else had missed it for 300 years. After studying thousands of shipwrecks, this was the first one Beeker had found that had not already been looted.

MUSEUM OF THE SEA

The ship and its contents will remain on the seabed as a "living museum of the sea" that can be freely explored by divers. The *Quedagh Merchant* gives divers a firsthand glimpse of what Kidd's pirate ship was really like. If Kidd did bury his treasure, it may still be awaiting discovery on a mystery island.

These are some of the remains of Captain Kidd's ship, the *Quedagh Merchant*.

BLACKBEARD AND THE PIRATES OF THE CARIBBEAN

EDWARD TEACH— BLACKBEARD

Born: Unknown

Died: 1718

Nationality: English

Probably born in Bristol, England, Blackbeard began his career as a privateer during the war between England and France. Many myths have been spread about Blackbeard, including that he had 14 wives.

A SCARY SIGHT

Standing more than six feet tall, with thick, braided black hair and a beard, six pistols strapped to him, and often lighted fuses burning under his hat, Blackbeard was the most feared pirate of them all. He even scared his own crew.

Blackbeard worked hard to make himself feared across the oceans. His victims would often surrender rather than face fighting this legendary monster and his 250 bloodthirsty pirates. In his short career, he captured more than 20 ships and became a legend as the most famous pirate of the Caribbean.

Blackbeard was the most famous of many pirates roaming the Caribbean and Atlantic in the early 1700s. Other pirates, such as Bartholomew Roberts, were less scary than Blackbeard, but just as successful.

Blackbeard was known to weave pieces of string or rope into his hair and beard and then light them during a battle. This would make him look terrifying!

THE QUEEN ANNE'S REVENGE

Blackbeard's career as a pirate captain began when he seized a French ship. He took the fast, well-armed ship for himself and renamed it the *Queen Anne's Revenge*. In this ship, he terrorized the coast of the Americas from Virginia to Central America.

Blackbeard made his base on the coast of North Carolina. Locals would buy the goods he stole from merchant ships up and down the coast. The state's governor was prepared to ignore the pirates as long as he got a share of their treasure.

BLACKBEARD MEETS HIS MATCH

Blackbeard did not care whom he attacked. He once stole the ship of his former friend and fellow pirate Stede Bonnet.

Other states were not happy with their ships being attacked, and so Governor Alexander Spotswood of Virginia ordered that Blackbeard's reign of terror must be stopped. Two small naval ships, commanded by Lieutenant Robert Maynard, were sent to find him.

Blackbeard used his knowledge of the coastline of North America (shown here) to try to outwit Lieutenant Maynard.

The two forces met at Ocracoke Inlet, in North Carolina. After a fierce battle between their ships, Blackbeard and his pirates boarded Maynard's vessel. Blackbeard was supposedly shot five times and suffered many sword wounds before he was finally killed.

Blackbeard's severed head was fixed to the bow of Maynard's ship.

"HERE WAS AN END OF THAT COURAGEOUS BRUTE, WHO MIGHT HAVE PASSED IN THE WORLD FOR A HERO, HAD HE BEEN EMPLOYED IN A GOOD CAUSE."

"BLACKBEARD'S DEATH," FROM CAPTAIN JOHNSON'S *GENERAL HISTORY OF THE ROBBERIES AND MURDERS OF THE MOST NOTORIOUS PYRATES,* 1724

BLACKBEARD'S TREASURE

When Blackbeard was killed, the only goods found were indigo dye, sugar, and cocoa. Blackbeard himself claimed that his treasure was hidden—but where is it, and why has no one discovered it?

One theory is that Blackbeard hid his treasure on the Isles of Shoals off the coast of New Hampshire. In 1820, a man working on a wall dug up a few bars of silver on one of the islands. Could they have belonged to Blackbeard? Despite many attempts to find the treasure, and stories that it was buried and guarded by one of Blackbeard's wives, nothing has been found since.

Maybe there was no buried treasure. Pirates usually agreed to split their loot among them. They certainly liked to spend what they had on wild partying. By the time Blackbeard was roaming the seas, trade in gold from South America was declining. Blackbeard and his men sold all sorts of trading goods in addition to the valuables they had stolen from passengers on ships.

"ONLY TWO PEOPLE KNOW WHERE THE TREASURE LIES: THE DEVIL AND MYSELF, AND HE WHO LIVES THE LONGEST MAY CLAIM IT ALL."

BLACKBEARD'S RESPONSE WHEN ASKED ABOUT HIS TREASURE

Although some pirates gained vast riches, many outlaws just wanted to steal enough food and other goods to continue their life of freedom.

On one occasion, Blackbeard's men needed medicine. The pirates captured a ship near Charleston, South Carolina, and threatened to kill everyone aboard unless they received a ransom and a chest of medicine.

SHIPWRECK FOUND!

The search for traces of Blackbeard and his treasure has not been totally wasted. In 1996, divers found a wreck off the coast of North Carolina. Although the ship was decayed, they were convinced that it was the wreck of Blackbeard's *Queen Anne's Revenge*, which ran aground in the area almost 300 years before.

One reason why the archaeologists believe they have found Blackbeard's flagship is because it is in the place where the ship is supposed to have run aground. The ship also has far more cannons than would be normal for a merchant ship.

In 2010, divers found an ornate sword hilt on the wreck. Could it have been Blackbeard's own cutlass?

An anchor was recovered from the wreck of Blackbeard's feared flagship.

The ship is a treasure trove of pirate history, but the *Queen Anne's Revenge* did not contain any gold and silver. No one knows if Blackbeard deliberately ran the ship aground, but the pirate and his men were able to move any treasure to another ship. Excavators have found only around one ounce of gold dust.

CANNON

Some of the cannons from the ship are loaded with small pieces of metal shot rather than cannonballs. These would clear the decks of an enemy without sinking the ship itself, a common pirate tactic.

Cannon cleaners

Restoring the artifacts from the *Queen Anne's Revenge* has taken many years of painstaking work. Seawater corrodes any items, such as wooden timbers, that are not buried in the sand. Cannons that have become encrusted with sand, seashells, and marine life have to be cleaned using chemicals over many years.

PIRATE SHIPWRECK: THE *WHYDAH*

Discoveries of pirate shipwrecks are very rare. Pirates did not use special ships, but rather any vessel they could lay their hands on, so linking a wreck to pirates can be very difficult. In 1984, diver and salvage expert Barry Clifford made an amazing discovery. What he found was not only a pirate ship, but also a ship that still had pirate treasure in its hold.

A survivor of the wreck of the *Whydah* (Thomas Davis) claimed there were 180 bags of gold and silver on the ship.

SHIFTING SANDS

Barry Clifford had grown up hearing stories about the wreck of the *Whydah*. He started his search for the ship by looking at old maps and documents that recorded the night it was wrecked on Cape Cod, Massachusetts. What the maps could not tell was how the shifting sands of the coast had moved or hidden the wreck.

The first cannon was found in July 1984, but Clifford and his team could not be sure they had found the right ship until a year later, when they found a bell bearing the words "Whydah Gally 1716." Since then, more than 200,000 artifacts, including gold coins, have been salvaged from the wreck, making it the only proven pirate wreck ever discovered.

BARRY CLIFFORD

Born: 1945

Nationality: American

He is a diver and treasure hunter who began his career as a salvage diver. Clifford was always excited by the prospect of exploring the wrecks off the coast of Cape Cod. He was rewarded when he discovered the Whydah in 1984.

The sinking of the *Whydah*

When a giant wave rolled the ship onto its side, cannons, cannonballs, and heavy barrels smashed through the decks.

The ship eventually broke in two and sank.

The main mast broke apart during the storm.

The hold contained cannons and treasure.

About 144 crew members died when the *Whydah* sank.

SLAVE SHIP TO PIRATE SHIP

The *Whydah* began its life as something even worse than a pirate ship. When it was captured by Sam Bellamy's pirates, the ship was returning to England with about $30,000 in gold and silver after carrying 312 slaves from Africa to sell in the Caribbean. Bellamy chased the ship for three days before its captain surrendered.

The pirates decided the ship was bigger and faster than their own, so they moved the rest of their treasure to the new ship. Some of the crew of the *Whydah* even joined Bellamy's gang.

The slave trade was big business in the 1700s. Many pirate crews included Africans who had escaped from slavery.

The legend says that Bellamy was returning to marry his sweetheart on Cape Cod when the *Whydah* was caught in a terrible storm. On April 26, 1717, the ship was driven onto the coast and rolled on its side. Only two of the crew members survived.

SAM BELLAMY

Born: 1689

Died: 1717

Nationality: English

"Black Sam," the captain of the *Whydah*, was said to have raided more than 50 ships in two years as a pirate. He died when the *Whydah* was wrecked.

"I AM A FREE PRINCE AND I HAVE AS MUCH AUTHORITY TO MAKE WAR ON THE WHOLE WORLD AS HE WHO HAS 100 SAIL OF SHIPS AT SEA AND AN ARMY OF 100,000 MEN IN THE FIELD; AND THIS MY CONSCIENCE TELLS ME."

SAM BELLAMY, AS QUOTED IN CAPTAIN JOHNSON'S *GENERAL HISTORY OF THE ROBBERIES AND MURDERS OF THE MOST NOTORIOUS PYRATES*, 1724

The gold and silver on the *Whydah* are just a part of the ship's treasure. More important is the glimpse of pirate life that the thousands of finds allowed. The artifacts from the wreck tell the story of Bellamy and his crew:

- Buttons, belt buckles, and jewelry show that the pirates' clothes were much more ornate than was normal at the time.

- Hollowed-out iron balls were filled with gunpowder and used as hand grenades to clear the decks of enemy ships.

- Pistols and musket balls show that the pirates fought their battles at close range.

- Bones of the crew are some of the wreck's most important treasures. They show that crew members included people from a range of cultures, from English sailors escaping from poverty to escaped slaves.

John King was the youngest of Bellamy's pirates. He was no more than 11 years old and begged to join the pirates when they attacked the ship he was on.

Searching the sands

The *Whydah* broke apart when it was thrown against the coast. The ship's treasures were scattered across the sandy seabed. The excavators used magnetometers to search the seabed for metal items. They also used special equipment that directs jets of water that disturb the sand and reveal the pirates' treasure.

Barry Clifford does not think of himself as a treasure hunter. He says he is a "history hunter" whose main interest is in bringing history to life.

These Spanish coins and a ring were found on the *Whydah*.

THE MONEY PIT

Just off the coast of Nova Scotia, in Canada, is an island that could be home to one of the greatest pirate treasures of all—or it could just be a natural hole in the ground, depending on whom you listen to.

The mystery of Oak Island began in 1795, when Daniel McGinnis found a shallow hole in the ground below a branch that looked as if it had been used as a pulley. With two friends, he started to excavate the pit. They found a layer of flagstones 2 feet (0.6 meter) below the ground and, 10 feet (3 meters) farther down, a layer of logs. The three continued digging. About 25 feet (8 meters) below the surface, they decided that they could not continue without help.

Could pirate treasure be hidden on mysterious Oak Island?

STILL NO LUCK

Digging began again in 1803, when a team of excavators dug to a depth of about 90 feet (27 meters), finding layers of wood and other materials as they went. Finally, they hit something solid, which they thought must be the treasure. Returning the next day, they were horrified to discover that the pit had filled with water.

"FORTY FEET BELOW TWO MILLION POUNDS [ENGLISH MONEY] ARE BURIED."

INSCRIPTION ON A STONE FOUND IN THE MONEY PIT DURING THE 1803 EXCAVATION. THE STONE HAS SINCE BEEN LOST.

Many people have theories about who built the Money Pit, from Captain Kidd and Blackbeard to agents of England's King George III. Some people even think it may have been built by Vikings, or even as a hiding place for a mythical religious treasure—the Holy Grail.

THE SEARCH CONTINUES

After 1803, many people attempted to find the treasure. They discovered that the water flooding into the pit came from a tunnel that seemed to have been dug as a deliberate trap to stop anyone from trying to solve the riddle of the pit. Shafts were dug and holes were drilled, but the pit refused to give up its secrets.

The pit has also claimed the lives of several treasure hunters. In 1965, the worst disaster at the Money Pit saw dig leader Robert Restall, his son, and two colleagues killed when they fell into a shaft and were suffocated by engine fumes from their drilling equipment.

Excavator Dan Blankenship prepares for another trip underground in search of treasure.

During the many excavations, a few artifacts have been found. Apart from the inscribed stone that has since vanished, three links of gold chain were found, but these have also been lost. The area around the Money Pit has now been excavated so many times that it is impossible to tell where the original pit was.

Shortly before his death, while searching for the treasure, Robert Restall was interviewed on a TV program. He said that he was sure that there was treasure on Oak Island. He thought that he could get it and would not leave until he had.

Dan Blankenship searched for the Oak Island treasure for more than 40 years.

Could X mark the spot? Treasure hunter Dan Blankenship claimed in 2003 that stones in the shape of a cross elsewhere on the island could reveal the true location of the treasure.

A PIRATE MYTH?

The Money Pit of Oak Island is often dismissed as a myth or even a hoax, with claims that some artifacts were dropped into the pit by local people to confuse investigators. Huge amounts of time and money have been spent excavating this small island. Could the treasure have remained hidden? Why has all the evidence to support the Money Pit theory disappeared?

Skeptics who don't believe the legend point out that the Money Pit could just be a natural sinkhole linked to an underground cavern, and that the evidence for the Money Pit is mostly based on old stories rather than hard facts.

WHAT DO YOU THINK?

If the Money Pit was dug by pirates, it was an amazing engineering feat. They only had picks and shovels. Despite this, they managed to dig the pit itself and the tunnels that would flood it without anyone knowing about it. Do you think there is still treasure at the bottom of the pit? Look at the evidence and decide for yourself.

The big dig

Modern technology has been unable to locate any treasure. In the 1960s, a huge pit was dug with earth-moving equipment, but nothing was found. Investigators now know much more about the rocks of Oak Island. Natural underground holes and caverns have been found elsewhere on the island and its neighbors.

Would pirates have dug such a deep pit for their treasure? Pirates who did bury treasure usually wanted to find it again quickly.

LOST TREASURE

No pirate's story would be complete without a tale of buried treasure lying unclaimed on a desert island somewhere. Many of these stories come from far beyond the shores of the Caribbean and North America.

CHINESE TREASURE

The seas around the coasts of China were a major hunting ground for pirates. Pirate queen Cheng I Sao and her general, Chang Pao, led a huge pirate fleet in the early 1800s. Eventually, many of the pirates, including Chang Pao, were persuaded to join the official navy. There are stories that Chang Pao buried much of his treasure in a cave on Cheung Chau Island, near Hong Kong. The treasure has never been found.

PACIFIC PRIZE

Cocos Island in the Indian Ocean is said to be the home of at least three different pirate treasures. The most famous is the treasure of Lima, stolen from the Spanish by Captain William Thompson in 1820. Thompson and his men were caught and sentenced to hanging. Thompson offered to lead the Spanish to the treasure in return for his life. When they landed on Cocos Island, the pirate and his first mate ran away into the jungle and were never seen again.

Cheng I Sao and Chang Pao controlled up to 1,000 ships and 80,000 pirates. Their fleet was bigger than many navies.

Policing the pirates

In the mid-1800s, navies began to use steamships, which did not rely on the wind and could travel anywhere. Pirates could not compete, and so large pirate gangs, living outside the law, became a thing of the past. Modern pirates still terrorize shipping in some places. However, the only things that remain of the romantic pirates of history are stories of their buried treasure.

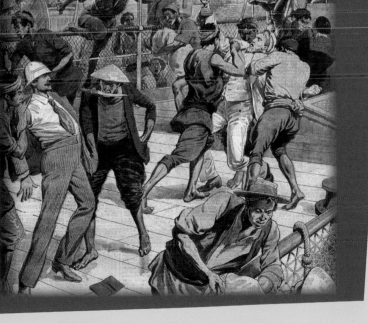

Chinese pirates attacked coastal villages and any ships that crossed their waters.

COULD YOU FIND PIRATE TREASURE?

This book is full of stories about pirate treasures, most of which have never been discovered. This could mean that they are difficult to find, but it could also mean that many of those stories are not true and the treasures do not exist.

It is romantic to think of pirates burying their treasure, but they probably spent most of their loot. Pirates did not save money for old age, as they were more likely to end their days hanging from the end of a rope or at the bottom of the ocean.

The team who discovered the pirate treasure on the *Whydah* spent lots of time studying old books, documents, and maps to help find its resting place.

There are plenty of stories of pirate treasure still waiting to be discovered, like the booty of Jean Laffite, who disappeared in 1821. Laffite's friends said he liked to bury treasure, but no one knows what became of him or his loot.

Treasure hunting tools

Technology can help treasure hunters. Metal detectors and underground scanning can locate treasures hidden deep underground. Sonar uses sound waves to detect items like pirate ships lying on the ocean floor.

While pirate treasure and treasure maps are hard to find, skilled investigators are finding out more and more about the life and world of pirates. If you want to find pirate treasure, you do not just need a taste for adventure. You also need to be good at following clues and solving historical mysteries.

TIMELINE

From 700 BCE

Ancient Greek pirates attack ships in the Mediterranean Sea.

Around 1100 CE

North African corsairs attack Christian ships carrying soldiers and goods.

1492

Christopher Columbus begins the European invasion of the New World. Treasure ships carrying gold and silver from the Americas to Spain are rich pickings for pirates and privateers.

1696

Henry Avery captures possibly the richest prize of all time when he seizes a Mughal treasure ship in the Indian Ocean.

Captain William Kidd sets out in the *Adventure Galley* to hunt pirates in the Indian Ocean.

1698

Kidd captures the *Quedagh Merchant*.

1701

Kidd is hanged for piracy.

1716–1718

Edward "Blackbeard" Teach's reign of terror occurs around the coast of North America.

1717

Captain Sam Bellamy's *Whydah* is wrecked on the coast of Cape Cod.

1718

Blackbeard is killed in a battle with Lieutenant Robert Maynard.

1720

Famous women pirates Anne Bonny and Mary Read are raiding ships in the Caribbean.

1795

Daniel McGinnis starts the legend of the Money Pit on Oak Island, Canada.

1820

Captain William Thompson disappears while supposedly leading Spanish authorities to hidden treasure on Cocos Island.

GLOSSARY

archaeologist person who studies the past by unearthing and examining historical remains

bloodthirsty fierce and violent

colony territory invaded or ruled over by another country—for example, as part of an empire

corrode become damaged slowly by chemical action

corsair sea raiders who operated in the Mediterranean

cutlass short sword with a wide blade, often used by pirates

decay rot

evidence items or discoveries that support or prove a theory or idea about history

excavate dig up

fund provide money or finance for something or someone

galleon large sailing ship. Galleons were particularly used by the Spanish as warships and to transport treasure from the Americas.

genuine real or true

gibbet cage used to display the dead bodies of pirates and other criminals

hilt handle of a sword

Holy Grail mythical holy treasure that was supposedly the cup Jesus Christ drank from at the Last Supper

indigo dye natural blue dye extracted from plants

knighted granted a knighthood. A knighthood is an honor given by British kings and queens to brave or loyal supporters.

legend story from history that no one can be certain is true

licensed operating within the law, with a licence

looted stolen

magnetometer piece of equipment that uses magnets to detect metals—for example, on the seabed

metal detector machine that can detect the presence of metal under the ground

mutiny rebellion against rules or authority, particularly against the captain of a ship

myth popular belief or story about something that is generally not factual

naval relating or belonging to a navy

ornate highly decorated

poverty being very poor

privateer private ship licensed by the government to attack enemy ships in return for a share of any treasure seized

ransom money demanded by criminals for the safe return of a person or object

salvage recover or repair, particularly relating to a sunken ship

sinkhole natural hole in the ground caused by water or rock movements that leads to an underground cavern

skeptic someone who does not believe, or is skeptical, about a theory or idea

sonar using sound waves to detect or map something underwater

theory idea of how something has happened

FIND OUT MORE

BOOKS

Clifford, Barry, and Kenneth J. Kinkor. *Real Pirates: The Untold Story of the Whydah.* Washington, D.C.: National Geographic, 2007.

Deary, Terry. *The Handbook of Pirates.* New York: Scholastic, 2006.

Malam, John. *William Kidd and the Pirates of the Indian Ocean* (QEB Pirates). Laguna Hills, Calif.: QEB, 2008.

Morris, Neil. *Pirates* (Amazing History). North Mankato, Minn.: Smart Apple Media, 2008.

Stevenson, Robert Louis. *Treasure Island* (Graphic Revolve). Mankato, Minn: Stone Arch, 2007 (a graphic version of the classic pirate tale).

WEB SITES

archive.fieldmuseum.org/pirates/index.html
Find lots of information about the *Whydah*, the pirates who sailed in it, and the ship's discovery.

www.mywonderfulworld.org/toolsforadventure/games/treasure.html
This is a great online game in which you find sunken treasure on the seabed.

www.qaronline.org
This is the online home of the project to recover and study the wreck of Blackbeard's *Queen Anne's Revenge.*

www.unmuseum.org/oakisl.htm
Read the story of the search for treasure on Oak Island.

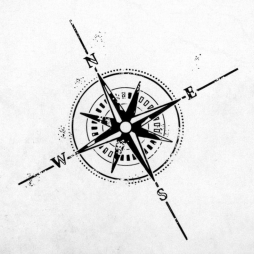

Places to visit

New England Pirate Museum
274 Derby Street
Salem, Massachusetts 01970
www.piratemuseum.com

This museum lets visitors relive the adventures of Captain Kidd and Captain Blackbeard. The museum includes a walking tour with a guide who takes visitors through an artifacts room, a colonial seaport, a pirate ship, and a cave.

North Carolina Maritime Museum
315 Front Street
Beaufort, North Carolina 28516
www.ncmaritimemuseums.com

This museum offers the permanent exhibition "Blackbeard's *Queen Anne's Revenge*," which offers artifacts and interactive features about this shipwreck.

St. Augustine Pirate & Treasure Museum
12 S. Castillo Drive
St. Augustine, Florida 32084
www.piratesoul.com

This museum combines artifacts and interactive displays to allow visitors to experience what it would have been like in Port Royal, Jamaica, during the Golden Age of Piracy.

The Whydah Pirate Museum
16 MacMillan Wharf
Provincetown, Massachusetts 02657
whydah.com

This museum is the headquarters for the ongoing archaeological missions to explore the *Whydah*. You can see the pirate treasure as well as artifacts.

Topics for further research

- *Life of a pirate*: Find out more about how pirates lived during the Golden Age of Piracy. How does it compare to the pirates you see in movies or read about in books?

- *Modern pirates*: Piracy is still a problem in some parts of the world. Look at newspapers and web sites to see if you can find out about modern pirates.

- *Pirate shipwrecks*: Find out all you can about shipwrecks such as Blackbeard's *Queen Anne's Revenge*. You may even be able to contact someone who has worked on unearthing pirate history.

INDEX